MAJORING IN MUSIC

LL THE **STUFF** YOU NEED TO KNOW

RICH HOLLY

Published by
Meredith Music Publications
a division of G.W. Music, Inc.
4899 Lerch Creek Ct., Galesville, MD 20765
http://www.meredithmusic.com

MEREDITH MUSIC PUBLICATIONS and its stylized double M logo are
trademarks of
MEREDITH MUSIC PUBLICATIONS, a division of G.W. Music, Inc.

Text and cover design: Shawn Girsberger

International Standard Book Number: 978-1-57463-150-0
Library of Congress Control Number: 2008942835
Printed and bound in U.S.A.

contents

acknowledgments

There are several people to whom I owe a great deal of thanks and without whom this book would have been impossible. I am deeply indebted to my research assistant, Kerry O'Brien, whose passion for the project and suggestions were invaluable to me and this book. A big "Thanks" to my readers: Dr. Laurie Piper-Elish (Northern Illinois University), Margee Myles (Northern Illinois University), Dr. Paul Bauer (Northern Illinois University), Dr. Kathy Hotelling (University of North Carolina), Dr. Harold Kafer (Northern Illinois University), and Dr. David Sweetkind (retired, Youngstown State University). And most importantly, deep gratitude and love for my wife and children whose support was instrumental throughout the book's preparation.

inTRODuCTiON

Congratulations! You may be reading *Majoring in Music: All the Stuff You Need to Know* because you're contemplating majoring in music in college, or because you've already made that decision and are about to — or just have — begun your undergraduate career. Maybe you're a high school student who is serious about music study and don't yet know what major you'll pursue in college. Regardless of why you're reading this book, you've made a great decision to go about your music study with as much information at your fingertips as you can get. I'm happy to tell you that the 4 (or sometimes more) years you spend as a college, university, or conservatory music student will be among the best years of your life. Expect to live in an environment that not only fosters you and your ability to develop and succeed as a musician, but also enables you to grow and mature as a person.

This book is divided into three sections: The Academic Stuff, The Musical Stuff, and the Life Stuff. Paying attention to all of these is vital to your success as a college music major.

Striving toward a career in music is a wonderful way to spend your undergraduate years. But you do need to know that pursuing a degree in music requires numerous hours of personal practicing and ensemble rehearsals, above and beyond completing the courses that are required for the degree. Be aware that in order to succeed as a music major you may commonly spend 12–16 hours a day in classes, rehearsals, personal practice and studying.

Of course, you or your parents may have questioned, "What am I going to do with a degree in music?" That's a valid question, and fortunately there are many great answers. It's beyond the scope of this book to offer complete career advice, but you can rest comfortably knowing that earning a degree in music allows you to not only perform or teach or compose music, but to gain employment in over 100 other music-related fields. There are also many happy and successful doctors and lawyers and businesspeople who earned their bachelor's degree in music. In fact, many employers like hiring people with earned music degrees, since to succeed as a music major means you understand how to work as part of a group, you understand focus and dedication, and you are creative. For more information on the wide variety of careers in music, you can visit your school's music library or purchase any of the dozens of books on this topic from your favorite bookseller.

My wife likes to kid me that my musical philosophy is "Peace, Love, and show up to the gig on time." Of course, I like to think that means that I am a responsible former hippie! But I think what it really means is that as musicians we have two responsibilities: one, as a caring human being, and two, as a responsible and prepared musician. Begin paying attention to details now, in your studies and your relationships, so by this time next year you don't even have to think about them — being organized and focused and thoughtful will just be a natural part of your everyday existence.

And most of all, remember to have fun. Yes, that's right, being a great musician doesn't mean you have to give up the things in life that you love to do. In fact, I believe that you must continue to be good to yourself in order to be a great musician.

SECTION I

THE ACADEMIC STUFF

Time management

Time management is a skill and perhaps an art. As a musician, you hone your skill to be better at your art, so time management is not really that far removed from what you do as a musician. For some readers, time management comes naturally, and for others, you will need to work at it.

Simply put, time management is nothing more than making a promise to yourself that you are going to make time to get everything done to the highest possible level of achievement in the time that is allotted to you. In an academic setting, that usually means both "What am I going to get done today?" as well as "What am I going to get done this week?"

A significant factor in successful time management is learning when to say "No." Sometimes you need to say "no" to yourself, and sometimes you need to say it to others (well, I recommend in those cases you say "No, Thank You."). The majority of students who become overwhelmed with all they have to do, and thus in most cases begin to suffer academically, musically, and emotionally, have not yet learned to say "no."

Here's a true story: A young woman, a music education major, was meeting with me and one of her music professors to discuss why she was not succeeding academically and what she could do in the future to insure better success. She was at a point in her academic career that if she had one more semester like the current one, she would no longer be able to pursue music as her major. It came out during the meeting that she, in trying to be nice to so many people, was saying "yes" all the time to "Would you play on my recital," and "How would you like to read some duets tonight," and "Can you give me a ride, I have some shopping that I really need to get done," and the like. She was in several ensembles, had a part-time job, and was enrolled in as many credits as one could have without it being termed an overload.

Her music professor and I tried several tactics to try to get her to understand how serious the situation was for her. She had one reason (read: excuse) after another as to why she couldn't say "No" to her friends and change anything in her life. Finally, I said to her, "But you have to realize, that by saying "Yes" to your couple of dozen friends over and over, your status as a music major is compromised, and consequently you are essentially saying "No" to the thousands of children who would have you as their teacher over the course of your teaching career."

Thankfully, that really hit home with her — her dream was to be a public school music teacher, and she was emotionally distraught at the thought of not being able to attain her goal. She was then able to learn to say "No," she enrolled in fewer courses and ensembles each subsequent semester, and she was able to accomplish all that she originally set out to do, all with much higher grades and greater musical achievement. Now *that's* time management.

Regardless of how naturally organized you might be, there is one helpful tool that I strongly recommend you invest in and use regularly: the day planner. Day planners come in many sizes and forms — from the checkbook-sized, pocketable version to leather-bound versions as large as a binder. There are many popular electronic versions, the Personal Digital Assistant (PDA) being the most common, but also smart-phones and software for your personal computer. All of these, regardless of cost, can get the job done. Most important is that you actually use whichever version you buy.

So, what is it you're going to do with your day planner? There are several things you are going to write down on each day of the current semester: your classes, your ensemble rehearsals, your meals, your personal practice time, your concerts, and your study time. But here's where it gets really important: every day, you need to do something nice for yourself, and this I like to call "Be Human." Schedule some time for you to do what it is you like to do that is not school or music related. It could be taking a walk around campus, playing racquetball, watching "Star Trek" (whichever version you prefer) or playing board games with friends. It doesn't matter what it is — if you like to do it, keep doing it regularly. And keep in mind that as incredible as it may seem, there really is enough time in each day to get done what you need to and what you want to, as long as you have practiced when to say "No" and when to say "Yes."

STUDY HABITS

How, when and where you study is typically a personal choice. There is no single method of studying that works for every person. Having said that, there are several tactics you can try. The goal is to have a plan for studying so that it takes the least amount of effort and time with the greatest possible results.

For some of you, you will have developed study skills in high school that work equally well for your college courses. For others, adjustments may be necessary from what you were used to in order to stay "on top" of your college-level work.

When you study is often just as important as how you study. Pay attention to how you feel at different times of the day. You may have a particular time of day that you feel tired, and other parts of the day in which you have plenty of energy. Make sure you schedule your practicing and studying for times of the day when your energy is peaking.

Where you study needs to also be considered. At your parents' home, while you were in high school, you likely and automatically retreated to the comfort of the desk in your bedroom to do your studying. If you can continue this practice in your college dorm room, then I recommend you do that. But you may also find that it's a very different experience. In a residence hall you don't have your own room, your roommate is always talking on the phone, the neighbor's music is coming through the walls loud and clear, and sitting at the desk just doesn't feel right.

If that's the case, I recommend you don't try to make it feel right. Chances are, you can't control either the neighbors or your roommate when you're studying, and trying to do so will just be frustrating for all of you. Instead, take some investigative walks through the campus buildings that you're familiar with — and if you're not yet familiar with both your school's music library and main library, now is the time for that. Most likely in one or more of these buildings you will find at least one spot that has comfortable seating and no one around who might disturb you. This then becomes your personal study place, and don't tell others where it is.

As for the *how* of studying, there are some standard practices for you to try. Some or all may work for you. Find not only a combination of these that works for you, but a particular order of that combination. That will help you stay on track and minimize the time it takes to study.

In no particular order, here are several techniques you can try in order to better remember and understand the material you're studying: re-write your class notes, either by hand or at your computer, which will cause you to give thought to them and perhaps reword them more clearly; highlighting pertinent sentences in your text book for future reference; as you read your notes and textbook, think of questions relating to the material (after all, tests consist of questions, so you'll be giving yourself a mini-test each study session this way); keep a log of your study progress; join with a study partner or group in order to assist each other; just as you probably used "every good boy deserves fudge" when you were younger to help you remember the notes associated with the lines of the treble clef, develop your own mnemonic phrases to better remember items.

One important item: if you are having problems with a particular course, don't delay in getting a tutor. For some subjects there are also subject-specific study tips. For instance, if you're struggling in your mathematics course, conduct an Internet search for "math study tips" and contact the mathematics department on your campus regarding working with a tutor and for even more information.

ADVISING

All college, university and conservatory music programs have a system of advising in place. I urge you to keep this in mind: Advisors are there to help you. That's their job. I don't think I can stress enough how important it is for you to see your advisor on a regular basis — at least one time every semester to make sure you are enrolling in the correct coursework for the upcoming semester. But many advisors can and will do more for you than just checking to make sure you're on track to graduate. It's a good idea to develop a strong relationship with your advisor so you feel comfortable going to him/her when you have questions that need to be answered.

Perhaps the single most frequent reason students go to their advisor is to drop or withdraw from a course. Each campus has its own use of the words "drop" and "withdrawal," so read your college's undergraduate catalog to learn what difference there may be between the two (on my campus, a drop permanently erases the course from your academic record, while a withdrawal is reported as a grade of W). It might be that you need to see your advisor in order to actually withdraw, or it might be that you need to visit a different office on campus for that. Either way, it's a good idea to discuss the matter with your advisor first. Advisors are trained to speak with about you a few pertinent issues surrounding dropping or withdrawing from a course.

Most significantly, before making a decision to drop or withdraw from a course, you must learn whether or not you need to maintain a full-time course load. You may need to do this if you are covered by your parents' health insurance policy, and you may need to maintain full-time status if you receive financial aid. Your advisor can help you with the details of your school's policies, and can make sure you know where you're going before you trek across campus to the financial aid office to ask questions of them.

It is possible to "self" advise, but I don't recommend it. In my 25+ years serving as an academic advisor as part of my faculty duties, I have met one (that's right, just one) student who self-advised and was actually able to graduate in 4 years. All the other students I have met who tried to self-advise found themselves in my office with the same story, which began "Well, I *thought* I was going to graduate this semester but I'm not." Meeting with these students is about the worst part of my job. In some cases, these are students who have already been accepted to graduate school or have accepted employment in an orchestra or other performing ensemble. Don't put yourself in that position — see your advisor regularly, and take the courses they tell you to take so that you can graduate at the first possible moment.

Campus Services

Your advisor can also help you to learn what services are available to you on campus. In addition, you can visit the website of the Student Services (or Student Affairs) division of your college to find out what these services are. I'll give you an overview of the types of services you can expect to find. The key is for you to recognize when you need any of these services, and then to actually go there and utilize the service they provide. These services are free of charge to currently enrolled students, and they exist solely to help make your life as a student more manageable.

The service you'll probably use the most is the Health Service. Later in this book, in the "Health" section, I'll discuss withdrawing from courses for medical reasons. Let's hope you don't ever need to do that. But you will get colds or the flu, you may come down with allergies, you may get some cuts or scrapes from a pick-up football game, or you may have some gastro-intestinal problems. Whatever the reason, don't hesitate to use the Health Service — you're entitled to use it, the cost of the visit is paid for by virtue of your student fees and/or insurance, and you need to feel better as soon as possible.

One campus service that is often overlooked is the office that helps students who have learning disabilities. Before I go any further, I want to make sure you understand that learning disabilities have nothing to do with intelligence. I can't and won't try to diagnose through writing this section, but if you consistently have the same types of problems studying, learning, doing well on tests, etc., then it's time you looked into whether or not you have a learning disability.

By federal law, should it turn out that you do have a learning disability, your campus is required to provide academic accommodations to you. It is up to you, however, to request these accommodations from each and every professor you have. I have seen many times that these accommodations work — students' lives are sometimes completely transformed once it's determined what their learning disability is and they start receiving the accommodations for which they qualify. If you suspect in the slightest that you may have a learning disability, contact the office on your campus that can help you with this and begin the process of getting an accurate diagnosis.

Your campus will undoubtedly have a counseling service available. In fact, some of you may have already utilized such a service and understand the value of the counseling service on campus. If you haven't used a counseling service before, I encourage you to use the services of your campus counseling facility when you're having emotional or psychological difficulties. When I meet a student who admits they are struggling emotionally but is thus far unwilling to go to a counselor, I tell them "Look, your need for a counselor is the same as a home owner's need for a plumber. You have to have one, you may need to find a second one because you didn't like the first one, but if you don't have one you're ultimately in bigger trouble and it will cost you even more money." If you recognize or even just think that your emotional state is not what it can and should be, don't wait — put this book down and go to your campus' counseling service immediately.

Other common student services include tutoring and workshops to develop stronger study skills, time management, note taking or test preparation skills. Most campuses also have resources for several specific populations, such as a women's resource center and a Lesbian, Gay, Bisexual, Transgender center. In addition, it's common to find resource centers for several ethnic populations, such as a Black Studies center, a Latino center, an Asian center, and the like. Remember, you've already paid for these services, so take advantage of them to be the best student and person you can be.

GET iNVOLVED

At my campus, there are over 200 active student organizations that are "recognized" by the Student Association. That means that these organizations receive funding from the SA for their own activities. Many departments and schools on campus have additional student organizations that are not recognized by the SA. Recreation Services on campus supports nearly 20 intramural sports, and intercollegiate athletics supports 16 competitive teams. The Graduate School supports hundreds of guest lecturers each year. The School of Music presents nearly 300 performances a year, the School of Art has 6 galleries with ever-changing work being presented, the School of Theatre and Dance has a new show just about every other week, and there are three museums on campus. I just love hearing a student say, "There's nothing to do around here!"

Studies have repeatedly shown that students who are active and engaged on their campus will have more academic, emotional and personal success.[1] Students who are not involved are making a choice to not be involved. Even if your natural inclination is to be by yourself, at the very least you can find some other music students who like the same kinds of music you do and you can start your own "club."

Clearly, there are plenty of campus activities for you to consider when deciding upon one (or more) in which to

---

1   Alexander W. Astin, "What Matters in College?" *Liberal Education* 79 No. 4 (Fall 1993) : 2.

get involved. Some will give you experience in a form of government, some will give you experience in education, some will give you experience in music settings. But what's really great is that all of them will give you experience in team-building and leadership, two of the most desirable traits when a prospective employer considers hiring you.

Many campuses host a day when student organizations set up tables and you can speak with several of them in one fairly short period of time. But through the magic of the Internet, most student organizations have information on your campus' website. Discover what the various organizations are about, narrow the field down to those you have interest in, speak with a representative of those organizations, and get involved.

SECTION II

THE MUSICAL STUFF

Practicing

I
t should come as no surprise for you to learn that many
music students choose music as their major because they
enjoy playing their instrument. It's what most of you have
done for probably 6 or more years before entering college,
and it's brought such joy to you that you've decided to pursue
a degree in music.

When you play music, there are only two types of settings
possible: solo performance and group performance. When
you engage in your personal practice time, it's important
to spend time on skills and literature that are applicable to
both of those situations. There is no way to predict right now
what jobs will be available when you graduate, so it's wise to
prepare for both solo and ensemble (and accompanying, for
keyboard majors) settings.

Much has been written on the topic of practicing. In fact, I
have seen entire issues of well-known music journals devoted
solely to practicing.[1] In this book it is not possible to present
everything I have ever read or heard in regards to practicing,
but what I will do is describe to you the method that I teach
and have had great success with personally and with my
hundreds of students over the years.

Because you will have a weekly private lesson, it's important
that you work into your daily and weekly schedule enough

---

1   "Inside the Practice Room," *Percussive Notes* 41 No. 2 (April 2003).

time to practice everything that you need to work on. This includes the music you're performing in your ensembles as well as the material your private teacher has assigned to you. In addition, I am a strong proponent of having a "daily routine" — a series of exercises and/or etudes that warm you up, refresh your memory (and muscle memory) of the major types of techniques required to perform on your instrument or voice, and in general prepare you for all your practicing and performing requirements that day. If you don't already have a daily warm-up routine, speak with your private teacher about setting one up that makes sense for you.

A question that is raised quite often is "How many hours a day should I practice?" The answer to that question is dependent upon several factors. In general, you need to understand the expectations of your ensemble directors and your private teacher in addition to your personal goals and expectations, and then practice enough hours in order to meet or exceed those expectations. You may not be able to do this in your first week or two of college, but within a few weeks you'll have a good feel for the expectations and consequently you can adjust your practice time accordingly. As a general rule, piano and string students can expect to practice up to 8 hours a day, while commonly woodwind and brass players practice only 2 to 4 hours a day. Percussionists have several instruments on which they must continually practice. I recommend a minimum of 2 hours of daily practice but 4 or more hours each day will allow you to become more familiar with more instruments and styles much more rapidly.

In my opinion, all student musicians should practice as often and for as many hours as they can. Yes, it's a balancing act with all your other responsibilities, but in essence you've decided to be a music major in order to become the best musician you can be. Make the best use of your time. What is likely to happen is that after you graduate and you're employed full-time either as a teacher or a performer or working in the music business field, is that there will be days when you cannot find the time to practice. And there are days when you might only have 30 minutes to practice. If you've had successful practices throughout your college career you'll be better able to work through the "dry" periods of practicing as a professional.

The system of practicing you're about to learn is designed to help you make the most of every minute of your practice time, so it isn't so much about how *long* you've practiced each day, but how *well* you've practiced. I'd much rather have a short, great practice session than a long one without focus or direction any day.

The first practice skill I encourage you to acquire is that of *Mental Practice*. In the Albert Brooks film "Defending Your Life" (Geffen Pictures, 1991), one of the story lines revolves around the fact that the character played by Albert Brooks only uses 3% of his brain. And, using as little of his brain as he does, his life has pretty much been centered on dealing with fear. Of course, this upsets the Brooks character, and makes for several funny lines in the film.

In addition to the great comedy in the film, what I like about that story line is that I believe it really is true of most of us — we are not using our brains to our fullest capacity. Additionally, if we overcome any fear of failure (or even fear of success) we may have, we will reap many rewards. Mental practice is one certain way to use more of your brain to insure more success in your music performances. And, the results of several studies show that including mental practice in how you prepare makes for better performance results than either mental practice or physical practice alone.[2]

Musicians, dancers and athletes[3] alike have found great value in incorporating mental practice into their routines. Some prefer a method of mental (or "motor") imagery, in which you visualize the motions you need to make to perform. Others prefer a method of repeating several details of what it is they're doing (for us, the music itself) to themselves. Both methods have been shown to be useful, and I encourage you to try both. Here then is the method I use.

When you get a new piece of music to learn, the very first thing you need to do is "read the words." By that I mean for you to sit in a comfortable chair (there's no need to be near your instrument) and look at — and talk to yourself about — everything on the pages that are not the actual pitches. What is the initial tempo? What is the key? What is the initial dynamic? Where are the phrase markings? Where do the tempi and dynamics change? Are there key changes? What is the range of the piece? By asking yourself these kinds of questions and finding the answers, you'll be mapping the music and you'll begin to get a sense of the form, the phrasing, and the musical ideas you want to employ when you perform the piece. Do this at least one time, but I personally like to do it 3 times so I'm even more familiar with the piece before I ever play a single note.

When I get to my instrument to begin playing the piece, the first thing I do is put the music on a music stand in its usual

---

2 Don Douglas Coffman, "The Effects of Mental Practice, Physical Practice, and Aural Knowledge of Results on Improving Piano Performance," (Ph.D. diss., University of Kansas, 1987), 101.

3 Shane M. Murphy and Kathleen A. Martin, *Advances in Sport Psychology*, ed. Thelma Horn, 2d ed. (Champaign: Human Kinetics Publishers, Inc: 2002), 405-406.

location in front of me, and I sight-read the entire piece. While sight-reading, I'll stop whenever necessary to make notes (with a pencil, on the music) about the places in the music that I know will be more challenging. When I'm done sight-reading, I place the music stand and the music off to the side, where I will not be able to see it while I play on my instrument. This begins the memorization process (which is not necessary for all instrumental performances, but helpful, nonetheless) and I do not learn any of the piece with the music directly in front of me. While this method may sound unusual, I have had great success with it as have many of my students and others that have learned this method.

In order to learn the notes, dynamics, phrasing, etc., I go to the music that is now off to the side, and look at the beginning. I make a judgment about how many notes I believe I can memorize without any problem. I don't want to short-change my ability, but I also don't want to overly challenge myself and not be able to play what I've chosen. I've learned what my limits are over the years and it only takes a second or two now to determine how much I'll work on at one time.

As an example, let's say I've decided I can play the first 6 pitches of the piece. In order to learn that small part of the music, I look at the music and talk to myself about what the pitches are, what dynamic I'll need for each pitch, what stickings (or perhaps for you, what fingerings) I'll need to use, and, what *feel* do I want it to have (more on this later). I'll then visualize my hands performing those 6 pitches on my instrument, which includes performing them with the correct dynamic. During visualization, I begin at a slow tempo and speed up as I become more confident about and familiar with the pitches. After only a few brief moments, I'm ready to turn to my instrument and perform what I've just practiced. Most of the time, my first performance is extremely close to what I want it to be, and I next physically practice those 6 notes perhaps 10–12 times to begin the muscle memory process. I then go back to the music on the side, repeat the process with the next group of notes, and so on and so forth.

There are two other keys to doing this: when you choose how many notes you will learn for each small segment, the final note of any segment you learn should be the first note of the next segment you will learn. This creates a very smooth transition from one segment to the next, and no listener would ever be able to tell that you learned the piece in such small segments. The second important aspect of this method is once you've learned two segments, put them together into a larger segment. When you've learned four segments, put those together into an even larger segment, and continue this so that you're continually lengthening how much music you can play without stopping. Eventually you will know the entire piece really well.

What I find so valuable about this process is that I am then able to "perform" the work in my head when I have a few minutes to practice but am not near my instrument. I can sit in any comfortable chair, close my eyes, and "see" my hands doing the work (or you can see your fingers doing the correct fingerings, etc.). I can practice anytime, anywhere.

The other method of mental practice is to repeat to yourself as many details as possible about each pitch. Here's an example of how this would be done: "The first pitch is an F, first space treble clef, it's mezzo forte, a quarter note. The second pitch is an E, right below the F, also mezzo forte but a crescendo begins on this note, and it is an eighth-note." You would recite such information to yourself in your head, essentially proving to yourself and any mindreaders nearby that you really do know your piece well.

Little by little, incorporate mental practice of each of these types into your routine. You'll soon find a balance of the two that works for you, and you'll also find that your physical practice sessions are more enjoyable and successful due to using more of your brain.

Now let's look at scheduling your practice sessions. As an example, I'll use the practicing requirements of a percussion student. This student needs to practice major scales and arpeggios, snare drum rudiments, timpani tuning, keyboard percussion sight reading, a marimba solo, and ensemble parts. Due to the course load the student is taking, there are only 2 hours a day available for practice. Yikes! How will this student ever get it all done?

By developing a systematic rotation of these requirements, by diligently utilizing a daily warm-up routine, and by employing mental practice, that's how. Of course, if the student has only 2 hours a day to practice, I would recommend they reduce their course load to be able to practice more hours daily, but in some music schools, due to the curricular requirements, this is not always possible. So, here's one possible rotation I would suggest to the student:

DAY ONE	DAY TWO	DAY THREE
20 minutes daily warm up	20 minutes daily warm up	20 minutes daily warm up
20 minutes scales/arpeggios	10 minutes mental practice on marimba solo	20 minutes timpani tuning
20 minutes rudiments	20 minutes physical practice on marimba solo	20 minutes sight reading
30 minutes timpani tuning	10 minutes mental practice on ensemble parts	10 minutes mental practice on marimba solo
30 minutes sight reading	20 minutes physical practice on ensemble parts	20 minutes physical practice on marimba solo
	20 minutes scales/arpeggios	10 minutes mental practice on ensemble parts
	20 minutes rudiments	20 minutes physical practice on ensemble parts

A rotation such as this allows the student to practice each specific item two times every three days, and breaks up each practice session so boredom and frustration don't settle in. You can employ this type of rotational scheduling no matter how many hours a day you have to practice. We've all heard it said: "Variety is the Spice of Life." I believe adding some variety to your practicing is good for all musicians.

And speaking of boredom and frustration, I believe there are two simple ways to greatly reduce if not completely eliminate both of those. The first is to *set small, attainable goals and reward yourself frequently*, and the second is to *strive for excellence, not perfection*.

In setting small, attainable goals, what typically works well are goals that are smaller than you might originally think. Many students have as a goal "I want to learn this piece of music." Certainly, that's a worthy *end* goal, but it does not have any value in terms of *how* you go about learning that piece of music.

In addition to the mental practice and physical practice tips stated earlier, it's important to be consistent with choosing and using your small attainable goals. Let's go back to those same 6 notes at the beginning of the new piece of music I'm working on. For me, that is a small, attainable goal. As ridiculous as it may sound, I never set a practice goal for myself that I don't believe I can't complete within 5 minutes. Of course, I call this my 5-minute rule. What those 5 minutes mean to me is that I choose my material to spend a maximum of 5 minutes on. At the end of the 5 minutes I am going to reward myself. If I achieved my goal in 5 minutes or less, then I achieved success and I deserve a reward. If at the end of those 5 minutes I did not achieve my goal, there are two things that occurred through the process: first, I am definitely closer to achieving my goal, and second, I just spent 5 minutes in great concentration and focus, and the combination of these two things deserves a reward.

My rewards are very simple, and I like to think of them as something I can do to be good to myself. My rewards are one of four things, or perhaps some combination of the four: leave the room and take a short walk, rest for one minute, drink some water, and/or do some stretches.

You can have whatever reward system you like, although I don't recommend that your reward be food (I know one student whose reward was a handful of little chocolate candies, and he gained about 25 pounds the first semester he tried this). And it should not be anything that lasts for several minutes. The point is not to disrupt your concentration and thoughts about what it is you're working on, but rather to celebrate your success so you're motivated to keep working.

I believe it's important to keep in mind that we all learn in different ways. While these short time periods of learning are very helpful to me, you may find that you prefer a longer time period in which you can concentrate, or even enter a "zone" in which you are strongly focused. It pays in the long run to experiment during your practice sessions to ultimately determine which approach works best for you.

I believe that perfection is not attainable by anyone, anywhere, at anytime. So don't even try to attain it. You're goal is excellence. Repeat after me: Strive for Excellence, not Perfection. Okay, let me hear you say it again now. That's it.

It's fascinating to me how many musicians could be labeled perfectionists. Unfortunately, because of their inherent perfectionism, they can never meet the impossible standards they've set up for themselves.[4] If you think you are a perfectionist, I encourage you to read a couple of books on the subject. In my opinion, they could be transforming for you, and you'll find that you reach higher musical heights with less work and frustration when you can let go of your perfectionism.

There are two other items that I believe are very important to your practicing, and the first of these is that every time you

---

4   Monica Ramirez Basco, *Never Good Enough: Freeing Yourself from the Chains of Perfectionism* (New York: The Free Press, 1999), 48.

play your literature in the practice room, think of that as a performance. Actually, it's important for you to put yourself into that mind-set *before* you actually play any notes. How you get into that mind-set is entirely your choice. I like to choose a specific thought, mood, or visualization for every piece and every movement that I play. That way, each and every day I go to practice that piece I can put myself in the same frame of reference which helps greatly in correctly reproducing all the musical decisions I've made, in recalling muscle memory for that piece, and in creating the aura and *feel* of the piece that I want for the audience to enjoy.

And the final item I'll discuss in this section is to find time each week to just simply have *fun* in the practice room. I have known many students who are so caught up in practicing only the materials their private teacher gave them, and worried that they won't have enough time to prepare those materials thoroughly enough, that they quickly lose sight of why they came to music school in the first place — because of the enjoyment of playing their instrument. If you have a particular style of music or a particular artist that you greatly enjoy listening to, why not also learn some of that music? Any notes and phrases and pieces you learn will contribute toward your overall ability and musicianship. And, so you know, over the years I have had a great time learning the music of Led Zeppelin, The Beatles, George Gershwin, Claude Debussy, Frank Zappa and others, simply because I wanted to. You need to practice music of your own choosing for the same reason.

Listening

Being a music major is an excellent opportunity to expand your listening skills in many situations. Of course, you've already developed some fine listening skills in order to become the musician you already are. Yet there are higher levels you can reach, and additional listening skills to develop.

I have found that many young musicians do not listen to themselves while they are playing or singing. That is to say, they listen but do not accurately hear the way they sound. You need to open your ears and be able to process what you're hearing when you produce music. One way to develop this skill is to sing a small portion of your music (one or two measures) several times so you have it correctly "in your ear." Then, play that same passage one time, stop, and think to yourself: "Did I just play it correctly?" (Note: vocalists can play their measures on a piano, then sing it before asking themselves how they did). Be sure that you're listening for the correct rhythm, the correct pitches, the correct dynamics, etc. When you're able to listen critically and successfully to just a couple of measures, then play longer phrases before stopping to ask yourself how you did, and eventually you'll develop the ability to be able to practice entire pieces and know you're critically listening the entire time.

You will undoubtedly spend many hours as a member of an ensemble. One of the most significant musical characteristics that makes a good ensemble become great is its ability to blend. Blend comes from a combination of factors, but listening is the first of these that each member must take responsibility for. It's imperative that you are listening to those closest to you as well as listening to the group as a whole in order to determine what you must do to make the group blend better. If you need to develop this particular listening skill, I recommend you find some friends with whom you'll play or sing duets, then trios, and finally quartets. By the time you know that you're listening well in quartets I would expect you're fully prepared to listen similarly in any large ensemble.

As a music major, not all of your experiences will be in producing music — you still have to take many courses. Developing good listening skills in order to understand your instructors and take good notes will serve you well the rest of your life, even though you probably won't be taking classes the rest of your life. But you will find yourself in meetings (yes, even orchestras have meetings from time to time), and on important topics like contract negotiations you don't want to leave a meeting wondering what someone said. To develop this kind of skill, most likely your campus offers workshops in classroom and note taking skills, and I encourage you to take advantage of those. But also, have you ever noticed a sign language interpreter? They must hear what someone else is saying and then repeat it back a couple of seconds later using a different language. And foreign language interpreters do essentially the same thing. You can practice this listening skill on your own by listening to books on tape, and repeating back what the reader is saying as an interpreter would. In class, you'll then be able to use this skill to help write your notes while the instructor continues to speak, and you'll retain more information overall.

I also encourage you to find time each week to do some listening to broaden your musical horizons. The music library will have thousands of recordings, all just sitting on the shelves waiting to be listened to. When I was an undergraduate music major, I discovered the joys of listening to many composers and jazz artists. In particular, I found "Concierto de Aranjuez" by Joaquin Rodrigo to be particularly relaxing. During times when I needed a break I would often go to a listening room in the music library, put on this recording, and lie on the floor and soak in the beauty of the work. After 20–30 minutes of that, I was always refreshed and ready to get back to my practicing or studying. When you find a recording that has meaning for you, keep listening to it and use that meaning to be a motivator for your studies.

USING THE METRONOME

I f you do not own a metronome, buy one as soon as possible. There are dozens of models available, and in the big scheme of things, it really doesn't matter which one you own. There are a few models that allow you to break up the pulse into subdivisions, and these can be useful tools. There are also drum machines on which you can program specific rhythmic patterns, which you might find helpful in learning some passages, and, these machines can loop rhythms which also makes a drum machine a helpful device. But even basic metronomes that only play the pulse allow you to do much great work with it, and that's what I'll concentrate on helping you understand.

Most musicians put the metronome setting at the tempo of the pulse at which they want to practice, and for the next several minutes the metronome relentlessly beats out time. Yes, this is one way to use the metronome, but it's actually not a way I recommend you use very often.

In my opinion, using the metronome in this manner makes the metronome a "crutch" — something you inadvertently come to rely on. Instead, I want you to think of — and use — the metronome as a "tool" that will help you to better understand time and how you maintain playing in time.

In using 4/4 time as an example, most people would set the metronome to click on each quarter note. But I want you to start setting it only on the half notes. You can practice with the clicks first as beats one and three, and then practice with the clicks being heard as beats two and four. When you're able to play in time doing both of those, then begin thinking of the clicks as the "and" of one and the "and" of three, and then as the "and" of two and the "and" of four. It's getting trickier, isn't it? But if you can continue to play accurately and play in time with the clicks being heard at those subdivisions, then you can really reward yourself, because now you are starting to get to where *you* are the one keeping time, and not the metronome keeping time *for* you. Ultimately, you can hear the clicks as "e" of one and three or "e" of two and four, and finally as "ah" of one and three and "ah" of two and four.

If your metronome is calibrated to go slow enough, I also recommend you have it click only one time a measure, using a similar system of hearing that single click as a different beat or as a single part of one beat per measure. When you can perform in time doing this, then you know you can play in time with the best musicians.

marking parts

I have met a few musicians who say they never mark their parts. But I can tell you that I know hundreds of musicians who do mark their parts, some of them so much so that you can hardly tell what the original music looked like.

Here's my philosophy on marking parts: the audience came to hear a great concert. If marking your part is going to help insure that you play to the best of your ability, then you need to mark your parts. Essentially, we all need to mark our parts.

Several instruments have symbols they need to use that are idiomatic to just that instrument (string players' bowings, alternate fingerings, percussionists' stickings and the like). Make sure you have your private teacher go over these idiomatic markings with you. But there are many markings all musicians can use, and I want to make sure you know what they are so you can start to use them if you haven't already.

V.S.	Write in large letters at the bottom right corner of a right-hand page, telling you to turn the page quickly! *Volto Subito*
//	"Railroad Tracks": abrupt stop. *Caesura*
	Draw a pair of eyeglasses to remind yourself to "Watch the conductor closely here!"
simile	Write this when you need to continue doing an instruction you've previously written on the part.
	Split long rests into several shorter rests, noting which player or section comes in at which point during the total rest.
	Circle items of particular importance, i.e. a new dynamic level, a new tempo, a key change, etc.
	Sometimes the words "cresc." or "decresc." get lost in between the lines of music. Draw in the graphic representation.
	If the next line of your music begins with a new dynamic level, write that new dynamic level in the right side margin of the previous line.
	Write measure numbers at the beginning of each new stave in all of your music.
w/saxes	Mark when you're playing (either in unison or in harmony) with another section or player so you'll know who to listen to and balance with.

music theory tips

O kay, raise your hand if you do this: You've just come out of your music theory class, and one of the first things you do is go to a practice room with your instrument (or piano for voice majors), and you practice what you learned in your theory class on your instrument. Go ahead, raise those hands. A-ha! I thought so. You don't do this, and hardly does anyone else.

But it is, in my opinion, a mistake to *not* do this. Let's go back to the number one reason why students choose to pursue a major in music — they enjoy playing their instrument. So, it makes a great deal of sense to use your instrument to help teach yourself all the concepts you need to know in order to fully grasp music theory.

Your private teacher already (I hope) has you practicing major and minor scales and arpeggios. In your freshman music theory course you will learn modes, and, just like scales, practice these on your instrument or with your voice. If your private teacher has assigned scale patterns and variations for use with major and minor scales, use those same patterns while playing the modes.

Pianists, organists, harpsichordists, and percussionists all have keyboard instruments as the instrument they can use to work on their music theory. The rest of you have a "single line" instrument or voice. So, while you might think those with keyboards have an edge when it comes to practicing the chords and 4-part voicings that you'll spend much time on in music theory, that is actually not the case.

Certainly a student whose major instrument is a keyboard can practice 4-part voicings from their music theory textbook by playing all 4 parts simultaneously, as the music was intended to be played. But I believe there is great value in playing each of the 4 parts separately, which all musicians can do. By playing one of the 4 parts at a time (in any register that works for your instrument or voice range), you'll gain a better understanding of the importance of melody within a harmonic setting. You'll notice more readily the suspensions, the resolutions, the appoggiaturas, and so on. If your major instrument is of the single line variety, practice as much theory as you can on your instrument or with your voice, and then go to a piano and use it as a tool to help you understand the harmonic elements.

As you learn more about chords and how various composers use them, you can practice arpeggiating them on a single line instrument as well as playing them as a chord on a keyboard. You can practice, for instance, how augmented sixth chords resolve by arpeggiating first the augmented sixth chord, then the I 6/4 chord, followed by the V7 chord, and finally the I chord.

As you practice your theory assignments more regularly, make note of other songs or pieces in which you may have heard that particular item used. Over the years I have found many popular songs that employ standard theory concepts, and you can do the same with songs you know. The work and joy of discovering those songs will make theory concepts really stay in your mind.

aural-SKiLLS TiPS

All college music curricula include course work in ear training, and these courses may also be referred to as aural skills. In these courses, you'll be working on your abilities to match pitches and to sight sing. You'll also be working on what's commonly referred to as "dictation" — the ability to hear rhythms, pitches and chords and be able to write them down on manuscript paper.

If these skills do not come naturally to you, there are some things I recommend you spend time on in order to improve your aural skills. First, sing. And then sing some more. Oh, and did I say you should sing?

I recommend you start by singing two things: one, sing music you already know, and if you have recordings of these songs, sing along with the recordings. When you know that you're singing the correct pitches and intervals between pitches, then go to a practice room with a piano and sing the melody, then find it on the piano (or use your own instrument or a guitar). Finally, write down the melody — pitch and rhythm — that you've discovered; and two, sing very simple and short phrases using your solfege syllables. Stay with just a few notes/syllables, so that you become very comfortable with the relationships between just those few. When that first group of syllables is comfortable for you, then work with another small group of scale degrees/syllables. And, you can also use your major instrument to help you hear the correct pitches.

Here's an example of staying with a small group of solfege syllables so that you become comfortable with and confident about them:

Once you've worked with several combinations of syllables you can start to combine some of the smaller groups into larger groups. And, don't forget — practice phrases that include leaps (i.e. Do Fa Re), since not all music is only by steps.

Sometimes you may hear the word transcribing — in essence, this means to write down what you hear on a recording, so it's much like what you're expected to do in aural skills class, albeit in a more relaxed setting since no one is waiting for you to complete it in a specified amount of time. Again, start with recordings of music that you already know, and transcribe various melodic passages. I recommend starting with songs that have simple melodies — just like with practicing and setting small, attainable goals, begin transcribing portions of melodies with simple structures. And when you first begin transcribing, be aware that the starting note can be any scale degree — don't expect the first note of the melody to always be the tonic of the key of the song you're transcribing.

MUSIC HISTORY TIPS

To be perfectly honest with you, I did not appreciate music history very much on either the undergraduate or graduate level. I did the work as best I could (not having much interest in it) and somehow earned decent grades, but I rarely approached the subject with any level of excitement. Nor was I "smart" about how I prepared for exams. Now, I appreciate it much more and find myself telling music history "stories" to my students on a regular basis. In addition to the sometimes "dry" information in music history text books, I've learned that the composers we discuss in music history class were *real* people with *real* lives, and I've found them to be, in many cases, pretty cool people. Based on this enthusiasm for the subject that I developed later in life, I'm happy to be able to tell you how to prepare for exams better than I was able to.

Every music history instructor I've known has put a list of required listening on reserve in the music library for the class to use. You must listen to recordings of all the music on the list, and be familiar with them in order to name them on the listening portion of an exam. Sometimes the length of this list makes it appear daunting, and that's because, well, it is.

But there is hope, and it comes by virtue of Modern Technology. Thanks to the abundance of compact discs and downloadable mp3s, you can have your own copies of all the required recordings. And, you *need* to have your own copies. I used to trudge on up to the music library (which was a fabulous facility that I often didn't appreciate) and spend hours locating vinyl LP recordings and listening to them as a completely separate activity. Many of you have a portable mp3 player, and many of you will have a compact disc player if not multiple players (car, home, portable). While you could think of some, there really are no reasons why you couldn't be listening to the required music several times a day without having to schedule separate time in the music library. You can be listening while you walk from one class to the next, listening while you eat lunch, listening while you do laundry or wash dishes, listening while you drive to go shopping, and so on. It's a fairly painless way to get a great deal of "home" work done without having to set aside time to do it.

Many music history exams require you to write down the years that composers lived. Here's how to better remember those years: when you first learn what those years are, go to an American History or World History book or website and find out what else was going on in the world those years. For example, let's say you want to memorize that Beethoven's "Eroica" Symphony was written in 1803. It will be much easier to remember (and meaningful) if you are familiar with Napoleon and post-French Revolution history. It's fascinating how much better you'll be able to recall composers' dates — and the other historical information — by actually making yourself remember even more information about those years.

It's often important to know in which countries and cities composers had active lives, and your instructor will expect you to be able to write about this information. I recommend all music students invest in a good world atlas when they enroll in their first music history course. Certainly, music history books are biased toward deceased European male composers, which sometimes limits the geographical aspect of music history courses. But more and more music history courses are including global information about composers and styles. No matter which composer you're discussing in class or reading about in your textbook, it's very helpful to also look at the maps in your atlas to see exactly where in the world this person was making their mark. By having that visual reference to where in the world each composer was working, you'll remember more about each composer.

SiGHT reaDiNG

I know that many of you came to your music school already a fine sight reader, but others may still need to work on this skill. In addition to providing tips for those of you who need some assistance, those of you who do well now in sight reading may learn something to either help yourself or to help a student you may have in the future.

Learning to read music is actually quite similar to learning to read a language. The letters and words in a book are nothing more than symbols that trigger your brain to tell you what that combination of symbols means and what it sounds like. You've learned to read both to yourself and out loud. In reading out loud, you've learned how to move your mouth and tongue to produce the desired sound or sounds. When you read music (again, symbols on a page), you move your fingers and/or hands (or mouth and tongue, if a vocalist) to produce the desired sounds.

The key is in training yourself to see music as combinations of the possible symbols, just as written words are combinations of the possible symbols (letters). There are 26 letters in the English alphabet, and only 12 pitches (17 if you include both common flats and sharps) in the music we read. Mathematically, there are far more possible letter combinations to form words than there are pitch combinations. As an example, there are 456,976 possible 4-letter combinations. By contrast, there are only 20,736 4-pitch combinations, and that number gets reduced to 2,401 if we're in a major key with only 7 distinct pitches. Think of how many words you know (okay, recent "expert" estimates show the average adult knows 50,000 to 75,000 words).[5]   And, because you know all those words, you can figure out how to pronounce (produce the sound of) new words that you may see.

So, ultimately music reading is far less demanding than word reading. There are two main reasons why your music reading is not yet as good as your word reading. The first is that you were brought up in a home and a school system and a neighborhood in which you heard words and used words all the time. It's doubtful that you played and listened to music for as many hours as you heard and spoke words. And secondly, it's simply a matter of your experience *working* on it: think about how many hours you spent with your parents and teachers learning how to read, and think about how you learned to read music. The number of hours spent actually working on reading music, for many of you, does not even come close to the number of hours you've spent working on reading words. Reading words with such fluency is often referred to as automaticity — the ability to perform a task with little attention.[6] That's what you need your music reading to be.

So, what are you waiting for? Get to work reading more music!

But hold on, hold on, you can't just start reading more music and expect to get better. It's very important, just as with all your practicing, that you approach this in an intelligent

5   Sebastian Wren, "Phonics Rules" *APA Online;* available from http://www.sedl.org/reading/topics/phonicsrules.html; Internet; accessed 5 June 2006.

6   Samuels, S. Jay. "Toward a Theory of Automatic Information Processing in Reading, Revisited." *Theoretical Models and Processes of Reading,* 4th ed. Ed. Ruddell, R.B., Ruddell, M.R., & Singer, H. Newark, DE: International Reading Association, 1994. 816-837.

manner that reduces or eliminates stress. And here are a few ways to do that.

When you began to read words, you did not start with a word such as "frustrating" or even "abysmal." Yet that's what your sight reading session will be if you choose to read music that is too difficult for you to read. There may be a fine line between sight reading music that is too easy, and perhaps boring, and music that is right at your level and even slightly above so that you are pushing yourself to become a better reader. If at first you're not successful choosing the right level to sight read, within short order you'll have figured out what music works for you and you can continue to grow from there.

So, where do you find this music? Why, your school's music library, that's where. Most music libraries will have hundreds and more than likely thousands of pieces of music just sitting there on the shelves, waiting for you to come along and sign them out. To get going with a regular sight reading routine, I recommend you plan on spending about an hour in the stacks of your music library with a note book, and keep pulling music off the shelves, writing down the call numbers of the pieces that look as though they would work for you as sight reading material. This way, as you complete your sight reading of one piece, you won't need to go hunt for another piece to sight read — you'll already know which pieces will work for you. When looking for music to sight read, keep in mind that you need not practice sight reading only with material that is for your instrument or voice — the music of any other instruments or voice that use the same clef will also work well. If the music you're sight reading goes outside of your instrument's range, just leave those notes out. You're practicing sight reading, you're not preparing the piece for a recital, so don't let those extra notes bother you.

So now you have music to sight read and you're ready to go. Here's what you do in the practice room: choose a tempo that essentially guarantees success in playing the correct pitches and rhythms (and hopefully dynamics, too). Just as when you were learning to read, your teachers and parents did not expect you to read at a particular pace — reading the word correctly was the goal. So do the same for yourself in the practice room. And it's perfectly fine to decide to sight read the music in small sections, just as an *early reader* reads short sentences. I like to jokingly tell my students that it's okay for the metronome to be set at quarter note = 1! If you need work on your sight reading, you're far better served by sight reading the music correctly at a really slow tempo than to be playing incorrect notes at a faster tempo. Success breeds success.

There is another method that I highly recommend you use in addition to the above. Most of this approach is found in the fine book "Music Speed Reading" by David Hickman. This book takes a novel approach to the development of your sight reading ability. What you'll find in "Music Speed Reading" are several pages of notes, but with no time signatures, clefs, or key signatures. This allows you to use each page many times, each time with a different key, a different time signature, a different rhythm, or even turn the page upside down.

There is one addition to what Mr. Hickman has you do that I would add. As in reading words, our eyes have been trained to recognize combinations of letters, followed by spaces. In order to train yourself to do similarly for music reading (and you do need to do this), I recommend you choose 2, 3, and 4 beat rhythms that are not a steady beat or division, but rather a combination of long, short and medium length beat divisions. For instance, in 3/4 time, you might choose to use the following rhythm, which you would then keep repeating throughout the entire page:

In this way, your eyes will connect (make a combination of) the sixteenth at the end of beat one with the 2 sixteenths and the eighth of beat two, connect the "and" of beat three with the next beat one, and your "spaces" will be beat three and the middle portion of beat one.

Sight reading can be challenging and it can be fun. Be smart about your sight reading practice and it will be fun and rewarding on a very regular basis.

Talk With Your Professors

Overwhelmingly, your professors will be more than happy to talk with you. It might be counter-intuitive for you to think this, but professors are people, and they have lives outside of the music school. It might be that some of your professors have the same hobby as you, or a particular professor might enjoy listening to the same obscure alternative rock band that you like to listen to. And, the more you get to know your professors, the better they'll be able to write a letter of recommendation for you if you're applying for graduate school or a job that requires recommendations.

If you did not understand something discussed in a class, later that same day go to speak with your professor about it so you understand it before you begin your studying for that day. If you are consistently not understanding class material, speak with your professor about tutoring. Either your teacher will do some tutoring with you or they can help you arrange to meet with an upperclass or graduate student who is an approved tutor for the course.

Some of your professors will be available for you to come in and chat with them about just about anything you want. Often you will learn a great deal from these sessions, as you'll gain much from the stories they have to tell, music-related or not.

And some of your professors will be excellent advisors, either (or both) academically or personally speaking. I encourage you to take advantage of any professor who is willing to speak with you at any time.

your recital

As you begin to think about and prepare for your recital, I highly recommend you keep this in mind: Have Fun! Preparing for a recital is a great learning experience as well as a time of much self-discovery: how you best use your practice time, how you organize and direct rehearsals for chamber music you may be preparing, what techniques need further honing, and the like. And, I expect you'll discover more about which music styles and composers are meaningful and bring joy to you.

Virtually all music degree programs require a senior recital. Many also require a junior recital, and some require a sophomore recital. Regardless of how many recitals you are required to perform, I believe it's in your best interest to perform as many as possible. Each year I meet a handful of students who are preparing their senior recital, and this is the first recital they've ever prepared. I believe this is a huge mistake, and I urge you to avoid that happening to you.

One of the most important things I'd like for you to remember is that as a student-musician you should strive for excellence. If your senior recital is the first recital you've ever prepared, most likely it won't be as excellent as it would be if you had prior experience preparing and performing recitals.

In my opinion, it's never too early to begin discussing your upcoming recital with your private teacher. Your teacher will help you determine when it's best to start working on it, but you can always discuss it sooner than that.

One key to successful recital preparation is discovering the balance between too much preparation time and not enough preparation time. This discovery process is one more reason why I recommend you perform more than one recital. If you begin preparing too many months ahead of time, there are two things I believe are not in your best interest. The first is that you may become bored or "burned-out" with the pieces you've chosen. The second is that any date on which you choose your music, those decisions are made based on your current technical proficiency and musical prowess. If you start recital preparation too soon, you may be denying yourself a few month's time to raise your technical and musical abilities. Taking some time to work on technique and musicality would likely lead to your recital material being more advanced and better performed. Again, discuss these issues with your teacher to determine the optimum timeline for you.

Recital preparation is the time for you to pull together and use all of the music learning techniques and tools you've learned in the preceding years: study and analyze your music, set attainable goals, practice mentally and physically, listen to recordings, and so on. In other words, be *smart* about your preparation.

The one area in which recital preparation commonly becomes frustrating is in rehearsing chamber music or other ensemble pieces. I've known of many students who agree to perform as an ensemble member on someone else's recital (and if you have that opportunity and the time, I encourage you to also do so). However, all too often, these ensemble members do not have the same level of commitment as you do (it's not *their* recital) and subsequently do not practice their parts often enough outside of rehearsals. This, of course, causes frustration for the person whose recital it is.

There are several ways to avoid this scenario. First, choose your players carefully. Among the strategies to consider are: sometimes your friends are not best suited to the part; students who have their own upcoming recital may be too busy and focused on that to truly commit to yours — although, you might be able to convince them to perform the piece on their recital as well; younger, eager players who might not have so many commitments may be an excellent choice; and hold one rehearsal very early on so you and the players know what you're in for. I also encourage you to speak with the private teachers at your school, asking them for recommendations based on the specific part(s) you need covered.

I love to use the phrase "target date." It's not an absolute deadline, but it is a date that you're shooting for. I believe you should aim for a target date of two weeks prior to your recital to have all your material prepared. In those two weeks leading up to your recital I highly recommend that you practice a little differently. You'll balance your time between fine-tuning sections of your pieces, running each piece from start to finish non-stop, and playing 2 or 3 "mini-recitals" each day. These mini-recitals are a way for you to get mentally prepared and physically comfortable with the logistics of your recital. You'll not play each piece in its entirety, but you will play the openings and perhaps endings of each piece, in the same order you'll be performing them on your recital. As well, practice walking into the practice room as if you're walking onstage. You'll practice breaks between pieces as you want to do them on the recital, and you'll also practice taking a mini-intermission. One final thing that I can't stress enough: decide what you'll be wearing on your recital two weeks ahead of time, and each mini-recital you practice you should wear the shoes you plan on wearing for the recital. As students, you're used to wearing sneakers and sandals all day long (heck, I would, too, if I could get away with it) and the feeling of dress shoes (the stiffness, the height of the heel) can be an uncomfortable feeling if you're not used to playing while wearing them.

Each day as you prepare for your recital, and most importantly on the date of your recital, do everything possible to make that day like any other day. You wake up, you get dressed, you eat your breakfast, you brush your teeth, and you play music. All of this is part of who you are. Try not to obsess over your recital by putting it up on a pedestal. It's not THE RECITAL, it's your recital. You'll be playing music like every other day of your life, there just happen to be some people there to share it with.

Here's another true story: One of my graduate students was a chain smoker and drank probably two pots of coffee each day. I had several conversations with him about his health. He did maintain an admirable weight and didn't seem to have any jitters or other visible symptoms of poor health. One day he showed up for his lesson and he was uncharacteristically on edge, and I asked him what was going on. His reply was "I'm in training. I stopped smoking and drinking coffee, and I'm getting up early and jogging 4 or 5 miles to start my day." I asked him what is it you're in training for, and he said "THE RECITAL! I figured I needed to be in the best health for THE RECITAL." I told him I applaud his health concerns, but that I was also concerned about him quitting smoking and coffee drinking cold turkey. I also told him that he'd be better served by not trying to adjust "who he is" while working on his recital — he should do that once the recital is over. He continued to not smoke and not drink coffee over the next 2 months, and one day he arrived at my office and announced he was canceling his recital. I asked him why, and he said because he's a nervous and physical wreck and there's no way he could prepare it in time. I believe for him it was a case of putting his recital up on that pedestal which led to poor timing of his decision to severely change his lifestyle. He wasn't being true to the person he knew himself to be, so he didn't know what a "normal" day felt like anymore and wasn't able to accomplish his goals.

Be who you are, make every day the same (which includes playing music), and just have a great time preparing your recital. You'll have a terrific and memorable performance.

ODDS and ENDS

What follows are several music- and school-related topics that are important to your academic success and musical growth, but don't necessarily require full sections of their own. I hope you won't interpret that to mean that these are less important, because that is not the case. Pay attention to and take advantage of the following as much as you would any of the information we've already discussed.

Compose music. If you haven't already been composing, start now. You will learn a great deal about yourself as a musician through the compositional process. You can write solos and etudes for any instrument or voice range, or duets, trios, quartets, big band charts, fusion charts, full symphonies — whatever you like. You get to experiment with how music can be put together, what instruments sound like when they're paired, and you'll learn how to put your ideas down on paper so they're played exactly as you intended them. Composing is a wonderful creative outlet that stimulates your brain in ways performing often does not.

Learn how to improvise. As with composing, you'll learn a lot about yourself and about how music works by improvising. And improvisation can be done in several musical styles — jazz, rock, baroque and contemporary music among them. Speak with friends who are experienced improvisers, or utilize the internet to locate resource and instructional books, CDs, DVDs and the like. I also recommend you find a friend of similar musical abilities to do this with — you can help each other and make a fun time of it.

Organize groups for fun and profit. Yes, whether it's a jazz combo, a rock group, a string quartet, an a cappella octet or a mix of instruments we don't have a name for, it's all good. In fact, it's all very good. By being the organizer, you'll be developing leadership skills. You'll have to hone your organizational skills. And you'll learn how to handle players that don't show up on time and/or have their parts prepared.

It's also important that you find performance opportunities throughout your community and surrounding communities, and through that process you'll come to understand negotiating the fee of the group and how to write up a contract that's fair for your group and the employer. By organizing your own group, you get to play the music *you* want to play, not the music a school or professional ensemble director wants you to play.

Be known as a flexible musician. Yes, it would be healthy for you to do lots of stretches daily and be physically flexible which would likely have some positive result on your ability to make music. But that's not what I'm talking about. The musicians that get hired again and again are the ones who can easily make changes and never complain about having to do so. When I was in high school, the band director had a sign on the wall at a level that was directly over his head when he stood on the podium. The sign said "Rule number one: The conductor is always right. Rule number two: If the conductor is wrong, refer to rule number one." You may not agree with what a conductor is asking you to do, and you may even have been taught by your private teacher to do a passage in a way that is counter to what the conductor is asking for. None of that matters. The conductor is in charge, and who knows, maybe what the conductor is trying to do sounds really good. Don't practice your ensemble parts so that you can only play them one way. Experiment in the practice room with them, and when you're in rehearsal you'll be much better prepared for anything the conductor asks of you.

Learn another instrument or learn to sing. You're going to be a music major for at least four years. What better time to learn about other instruments or to learn to sing if you haven't already done that. You'll be friends with music students who play and sing all sorts of instruments and musical styles. I recommend that you barter with one of them each semester you're in school and teach each other your instrument or voice. The time it takes to practice a new instrument or practice singing is time well-spent. Sure, you have to find that time, but through those experiences you'll become a richer, broader musician capable of finer performances on your major instrument.

Take care of your instrument. There are those of you who will attend music school with a really fine instrument that may serve you well the rest of your life. And there are those of you who will need to purchase a new instrument if you are to really progress in your performance studies. If the instrument you're playing is not the level of instrument you ultimately want or need to own, speak with your private teacher about what instruments s/he recommends, and begin making plans as soon as possible to save the money you'll need to buy a great instrument.

But regardless of how great your instrument may or may not be, you must take care of it. If your private teacher in high school or earlier did not teach you how to care for your instrument, speak with your private teacher about how to do that. You need that instrument to last many years and serve you well several hours every day (come to think of it, it's much like brushing your teeth in that way). And if you're a vocal major, your voice is your instrument, and you need to know how to take care of your voice. Make sure you learn how to do that in the first few weeks of your freshman year so you can stay vocally healthy day in and day out.

There are also those among you that will not be playing your own instrument. Pianists, percussionists, harpsichordists, and organists will be *using instruments that the school owns.* Additionally, there may be those among you who are, say, string bass majors who have yet to find and purchase a fine instrument and will be using a school-owned instrument until that time comes. It is so important that you treat these instruments as if they were your own. Undoubtedly, something will go wrong with one of these instruments, and it's imperative that you let your private teacher and/or the school's instrument technician know immediately when a repair needs to be made. The sooner the repair can be made, the less inconvenience there is to you and the others using that instrument.

Join your professional societies. Vocalists and all instrumentalists have their own professional societies. These organizations exist to serve the members, that is, to provide education, information and outlets for growth so that each member can grow their career in as many ways as they would like. The sooner you join, the sooner you will know more about your instrument's history, literature, pedagogy, major artists and technique. If you want to be successful in a music career, join your professional society and become active in it. Your private teacher can tell you more about your society, and how you can join.

In addition to joining the society for your instrument or voice, music education majors are encouraged to join the Music Educators National Conference (MENC), the professional society for music educators. Jazz students should purchase a subscription to *JAZZed* magazine. I recommend that vocalists who expect to direct choirs join the American Choral Directors Association (ACDA). And instrumentalists who expect to direct bands will be well-served by joining the College Band Directors National Association (CBDNA).

SECTION III

THE LIFE
STUFF

Embracing a Positive Attitude

I f there is only one thing you take away from having read this book, knowing that you need to develop and maintain a positive attitude is that one thing. This trait will serve you well — indeed, very well — your entire life, no matter what directions your life and career take.

The power of a positive attitude has been well-documented. Generations were raised knowing the effects of "The Power of Positive Thinking" by Norman Vincent Peale (Prentice-Hall, 1952). Anthony Robbins is a one-man international star and corporation because of his positive attitude and ability to instill that in others. An entire industry — motivational speaking — has thrived based on how effective a positive attitude is.

Perhaps you've noticed — throughout this book I've used the words "joy" and "enjoy" frequently. This is why we play music. We *play* music, we don't *work* music. And when you do something that you greatly enjoy, when you *play*, it brings with it a warm, good feeling. You have the ability to turn that personal, warm feeling into a positive attitude and keep it with you wherever you go and in whatever you do. And I also believe you have an obligation to share that attitude with those around you.

Perhaps you've heard this "light bulb" joke before: How many percussionists does it take to change a light bulb? Ten. One to change the bulb, and nine to stand around saying, "Big deal. I could do it better than that." The one changing the light bulb likely has a positive attitude and the nine standing around and criticizing clearly have bad attitudes.

If a teacher or conductor asks for a volunteer, do you jump at the chance to be the one "changing the light bulb?" Or do you prefer to sit back and criticize the volunteer? When a stand-mate is having difficulties with a passage, do you stay quiet and relish in the thought that you're not having difficulties? Or do you gently assist your mate with helpful tips on how to play that passage?

I'm reminded of two great examples of using a positive attitude to create something extremely powerful. The first is when producer extraordinaire Quincy Jones recorded "We Are The World" (Columbia Records, 1985) with a bevy of international stars in order to raise funds for drought-stricken Ethiopia. Jones was questioned about how he was able to get so many big name singers to work together so well in such a short period of time to make such a successful recording. He stated that at the entrance to the recording studio, he taped a sign saying "check your ego at the door."

The second example is the 2008 U.S. Olympic basketball team. For many years, this team was nicknamed "The Dream Team," due to the roster being completely populated with NBA stars. In 2004, however, the team did not live up to its billing — 10 of the 12 original players bowed out prior to the Olympics, forcing the U.S. to find last-minute replacements. That year's team lost more games than any other U.S. men's basketball team. However, because of that year's team, USA

Basketball sought players who would make a three-year commitment culminating in the 2008 Olympics. Because several high-profile players decided to "check their egos at the door" and play for the U.S. team for three years straight, the 2008 Olympic team brought home the gold, winning all of its games by a nearly 30-point average.

In the music world, no matter which facet of it you pursue, you will be a member of a team. Even successful solo artists have a team — managers, agents, wardrobe consultants, lawyers, etc. To be at the top of your game, you need to know how to work as a team member — how to maintain and use that positive attitude at all times. As a public school music teacher your attitude will rub off on your students. As a section member of an orchestra those around you will notice and react to you based on your attitude. As an employee of a large music corporation you'll be speaking and meeting with dozens of people each and every week. Your attitude will determine how far you get in the business, regardless of which part of the music business you're in.

Howard Schultz, the famed CEO of Starbucks who built the company from a single store to the international corporate giant it is today, says it beautifully: "Success should not be measured in dollars: It's about how you conduct the journey, and how big your heart is at the end of it."[1] When you play music and interact with others, remember and feel the joy, and let your positive attitude steer you in the right directions.

1   Howard Schultz and Dori Jones Yang, *Pour Your Heart Into It: How Starbucks Built a Company One Cup at a Time* (New York: Hyperion, 1997), 337.

HEALTH

I know you've heard this said but I'll say it again: Your health is the most important thing. This is not just some time-worn cliché, it is the truth. And let me be clear: in this section, the words health and medical are referring to both psychological as well as physical health.

As a university administrator, one of my duties is to speak with students who are unable to attend classes due to health problems. Some semesters it astonishes me how many students are in this situation. But even more troubling are the students who ignore the tell-tale signs of sickness and convince themselves that they will magically get better on their own.

I can tell you — utilizing that philosophy is *not* in your best interest. What happens in all too many of these cases is the student's health deteriorates further, they cannot continue to attend classes and complete the coursework, and their permanent university record displays low grades.

All colleges and universities have a system for withdrawing due to medical reasons. If you are unable to attend class due to medical reasons, it is very important to get an early diagnosis and subsequent treatment from a physician, either at your campus health service or through a private practice. I also recommend you contact your advisor to discuss your withdrawal options and the procedure you must then follow.

Your overall, general health is of the utmost importance. As was discussed earlier in the Study Habits section of this book, you may find that you are tired at a re-occurring time each day. If you have more than one time each day in which you feel tired, then I recommend a trip to your physician, getting more exercise, getting more rest/sleep, changing your diet, or some combination of these.

It's important that you engage in some form of exercise on a regular basis, which can be as simple as a long walk several times a week or as regimented as weight-training and/or aerobics sessions every day. It can also be through your participation in an intramural sport, or frequent biking, rollerblading, jogging, softball with friends, etc. It doesn't matter what it is, what does matter is that you find a physical activity you like and make it part of what you do on a regular basis.

Getting enough sleep is often overlooked by college students, but it is an essential part of your overall health. The National Sleep Foundation (www.sleepfoundation.org) recommends that going to bed at a similar time each night, getting 7-9 hours of sleep, and waking up at a similar time each morning will provide you with enough sleep so that you function at your fullest capacity.

One of the phrases that's commonly discussed is the "freshman fifteen." This refers to college freshmen and women gaining fifteen pounds. Although recent research has shown this to not be true, it can be true that maintaining a nutritionally sound diet may be difficult.[2] Additionally, most nutritionists agree, it's just as important that you eat three balanced meals a day. Pay attention to what and how

2   Carole Nhu'y Hodge, Linda A. Jackson, and Linda A. Sullivan, "The 'Freshman 15': Facts and Fantasies About Weight Gain in College Women," *Psychology of Women Quarterly* 17 (1993) :119.

much you're eating. To be alert 16 hours a day in classes, rehearsals, practice sessions and study time, you need to be in good health.

roommates

As a student in most colleges, you will be assigned a roommate by the staff of the campus housing office. How they determine who will live with who is a great mystery. For some roommates it works out beautifully, for others it can be a horrible experience.

Of course, I hope that your roommate and you get along well and can coexist without any problems. But if you are having problems, you must do something about it.

Each campus will have its own policies and regulations for how you go about switching roommates, so you need to inquire about those policies so that you understand what your options and rights are. Before you pursue moving out of your assigned room, I encourage you to speak with the residence hall staff and/or the university ombudsman, all of whom are trained to assist with conflict resolution. The ombudsman's job is to help facilitate communication and if necessary mediate a resolution between members of your college or university. Seeing your ombudsman is free of charge, and rest assured they will help you in a completely confidential manner to find a workable solution to your roommate problem. Working out the differences you and your roommate are experiencing may be all that you need.

CHOOSING
FRiENDS

O ne of the greatest things about being a college
student is all the wonderful people you will
meet, many of whom will become friends for life.
Unfortunately, there are some college students who are
not so wonderful and may be inclined to commit crimes
(obviously, stay away from them). There are some college
students who are well-intentioned but are "high maintenance"
and having a relationship with them will eat up all your
time (be honest with them and tell them you cannot spend
that much time with them). There are also students who
are having psychological problems and may come to you for
solace. To best help these friends, you might consider walking
them over to your campus counseling service so that they
receive professional help.

Think about the friends you had in high school. Most likely,
you had much in common with them in terms of likes and
dislikes (music, fashion, sports, politics, religion, chess,
what have you). But also think about your friends' level of
dedication to their studies and ability to focus. If you can
honestly say that your high school friends had the same
dedication and focus as you, which I hope were both high,
then you already have a good track record of choosing friends.

I meet regularly with students who tell me they are not
getting their work done because their friends constantly

pressure them into joining them in some social activity, and the student feels obliged to go with them. If this is the case with you, then it becomes very important that you tell your friends that you're not getting your school work done and you need to study/practice more. If they are really your friends, they will understand and you'll see no difference in the way they treat you. If they have a problem with you being honest with them, and become negative, then perhaps they are not the best choices of friends for you.

money

Personal finance expert Suze Orman says that money is the number one reason why couples argue. Health and wellness educator Terra Wellington reports that for the majority of people, money and finances are two of the most stressful factors in life. And according to a 2004 survey administered by the American Psychological Association, almost 75% of those who responded claimed that money was the number one cause of stress for them.

Of course, in college, you have tuition, room and board expenses, student fees, the cost of text books, music purchases, other music supply needs based upon your major instrument, and a desire and probably a need for weekly spending money. To be honest, about the last thing you need in addition to your course work, practicing and studying is to have financial worries.

Some of you will have all your education-related costs paid for by your parents. On the opposite end of the spectrum, some of you will be working part- or maybe even full-time in order to pay your school expenses. And some of you will work hard and for long hours in the summers so you can save money to have while you're at school the other 9 months of the year.

Here's another true story: One of my students decided it was time to join a rock band, get some experience doing that, and make money while he was at it. The band he joined rehearsed 40 miles away from our campus. The student had to buy a car in order to get to these rehearsals and ultimately gigs.

In the meantime, to pay off the loan on the car, he had to take a job at a fast-food restaurant working 20-25 hours a week. He began eating 2 or more meals a day in the fast food restaurant.

So, literally overnight, here was a student who went from having a week consisting of a full-time course load, rehearsals for two school ensembles, private practice time and study time, to a schedule that included all that *plus* 20+ hours a week of work, 15+ hours a week driving to and from and the playing in rehearsals and/or gigs, and eating most of his meals in a not very nutritionally sound manner. As you may have guessed, his school work and personal practicing went completely downhill, he gained a great deal of weight, and was constantly overstressed.

What this student failed to do was to seriously consider how the money came into play in his decision to join that particular rock band. To him, he was making a decision about an experience he wanted as a musician. While that's partially true, what he had also done is turn his finances completely upside down and subsequently his studies and health, as well.

What I hope you learn from this is that before you agree to adding something to your life as a college music major, you need to take some time to think through whether this decision will positively or negatively affect your financial situation. Just because you may make some money performing doesn't mean that in the big picture it's good for your pocketbook, or, as in the case above, your health and well-being. The same consideration is for those of you working to pay your school bills. You need to seriously consider how many classes/credits you can successfully carry in a semester if you are working at a job so many hours each week. Do yourself a favor, and remember, as we discussed in the Time Management section, to say "No." Don't overdo it.

Then there's the financial aid part of the equation. Many of you will be receiving financial aid in order to pay your college expenses. Financial aid comes in three basic forms: talent or academic scholarship awards, grants, and loans. By the time you are enrolled in courses, you and your family will likely know what your financial aid package will be and will begin to make plans to pay for your education.

The federal government, in conjunction with state governments, enforces a group of policies that govern not only who qualifies for financial aid to begin with, but also how a qualified student *remains* qualified semester after semester. On many campuses, this is referred to as financial aid Satisfactory Academic Progress (SAP) or Reasonable Academic Progress (RAP). Each campus may develop its own system of dealing with students who do not meet SAP/RAP status, but there are a few generalities you should know.

In order to remain eligible for financial aid, you will likely need to (1) maintain at least a 2.00 Grade Point Average, (2) pass more than 2/3 of your courses, and (3) have attempted no more credits than what would be 150% of the total credits required for your degree program. If you are a student receiving any kind of financial aid (and that means 70% of you), I strongly urge you to contact the financial aid office on your campus if you have any questions regarding your financial aid package, your eligibility, or any other related issue.

alcohol and drugs

The legal drinking age in all 50 of the United States is 21, and the peer pressure to drink alcohol before age 21 is often very strong. And although they are illegal substances, you will likely meet students who encourage you to use drugs.

Most (and possibly all) college campuses have help for students with questions or concerns about alcohol and drugs. Before you make a decision whether or not to drink alcoholic beverages or use illegal drugs, it's a good idea to understand the answers to your questions and to gather as much information as possible. Check your college's website for this kind of information, or contact the Student Affairs office on campus. You need to be fully informed about the legal ramifications as well as the physical and psychological effects drugs or alcohol would have on you, and make sure you understand your campus' policies before you make a decision. I encourage you to keep in mind this simple and true statement: *one poor choice can ruin your life.*

I can tell you that every year, students leave college due to problems with drinking alcohol and/or using drugs. Very few things are sadder for me than to see a talented, intelligent young musician either be academically dismissed from school or have such serious health problems that they must leave school due to their drug or alcohol use.

Music students come to school very excited about their college career and what the future holds for them, and if the wrong decisions are made, that future can be put in jeopardy. I can't tell you what to decide, but I will encourage you to speak with your parents, speak with a counselor on your campus, speak with a member of the clergy or speak with an older relative you admire. Be informed, and make smart decisions so that one day, we can count you among the vibrant members of the professional music world.

sexual relations

Perhaps this topic is just as difficult as alcohol and drugs, but you must, at the very least, think about it. Understanding the topic of sexual relations is important for all students regardless of sexual orientation. By now, I hope you know that if you do choose to have sexual relations while in college, you need to have protected sex, whether you are gay, straight, or bisexual.

But there are additional issues you need to know about and be ready to make decisions about. Do you understand what consent to having a sexual relationship means? Do you know the many definitions of rape? These definitions refer to more than only penetration by a man to a woman. Rape and sexual assault are defined by law, and consent (or lack thereof) is a defining factor in rape situations. Have you determined and are no longer struggling with your own sexuality? Do you understand what sexual harassment is? What effects might drugs or alcohol have on your sexual relations? Are you prepared for the ramifications of you or your partner becoming pregnant?

Be aware that college and university campuses are not immune to cases of domestic violence, date violence, stalking and cyber stalking. While not always of a sexual nature, these instances do often result from a relationship into which you entered. Make sure you really know the person you are with before committing to a sexual relationship.

Thankfully, your campus will have resources available to help you learn the answers to these questions and to help you make the best decision you can for yourself and even for your partner. It's in your best interest to be fully informed before you decide about sexual relations for yourself.

BE GOOD TO YOURSELF

To reiterate what was said back in the Introduction, you must be good to yourself if you wish to succeed. I'd like for you to keep two things in mind. First, your college transcript (the official recording of your grades) follows you for the rest of your life. You need to have it look as good as possible for those jobs or graduate schools you may apply for that require one. And second, musicians most often get hired based on the level of achievement and musicality they can demonstrate either through an audition, portfolio, or resume (also known as a vita, or curriculum vita, or C.V.).

To have your transcript look good or even great, and to be the best musician you can possibly be when you graduate, you need to be good to yourself. Eat correctly, get some exercise, get enough rest, deal with stress, be smart about alcohol and drugs, get help when you need it, ask lots of questions, and don't be in a rush to graduate. Many of you will indeed graduate in four years, but many of you will take five years to complete your program. It doesn't matter to an employer or a graduate school how old you are when you graduate. They're looking for the best musician with the best transcript and best level of maturity and responsibility. So if staying in school one more year will help either or both your level of musicianship or the grades on your transcript, then I would encourage you to strongly consider taking that extra year to earn your degree. And remember: Peace, Love, and show up to the gig on time.

references

"As Tax Deadline Approaches Americans Say Money is Number One Cause of Stress" [Article, March 31, 2004]. *American Psychological Association Press Release.* Available from http://www.apa.org/releases/moneystress.html. Internet. Accessed 5 July 2006.

Astin, Alexander W. "What Matters in College?" *Liberal Education* 79 No. 4 (Fall 1993) : 4–16.

Basco, Monica Ramirez. *Never Good Enough: Freeing Yourself from the Chains of Perfectionism.* New York: The Free Press, 1999.

Chickering, Arthur W. and Zelda F. Gamson. "Seven Principles for Good Practice in Undergraduate Education" [Article, March 1987]. *American Association for Higher Education Bulletin.* Available from http://www.csueastbay.edu/wasc/pdfs/End%20Note.pdf. Internet. Accessed 5 July 2006.

Coffman, Don Douglas. "The Effects of Mental Practice, Physical Practice, and Aural Knowledge of Results on Improving Piano Performance." Ph.D. diss., University of Kansas, 1987.

Defending Your Life. Prod. Herbert S. Nanas. Dir. Albert Brooks. Perf. Albert Brooks, Meryl Streep, Rip Torn, and Lee Grant. DVD. Geffen Pictures, 1991.

Freymuth, Malva. *Mental Practice and Imagery for Musicians: A Practical Guide for Optimizing Practice Time, Enhancing Performance, and Preventing Injury.* Colorado: Integrated Musician's Press, 1999.

Galvan, Mary G. "Kinesthetic Imagery and Mental Practice: Teaching Strategies for the Piano Principal." Ph.D. diss., University of Miami, 1992.

Gille, Susan V. "The Influence of Social and Academic Integration and Use of Campus Resources on Freshman Attrition." Ph.D. diss., University of Missouri-Kansas City, 1985.

Hickman, David R. *Music Speed Reading*. Century City, CA: Wimbledon Music, Inc., 1979.

Hodge, Carole Nhu'y, Linda A. Jackson, and Linda A. Sullivan. "The 'Freshman 15': Facts and Fantasies About Weight Gain in College Women." *Psychology of Women Quarterly* 17 (1993), 119–126.

Kuhn, Melanie R. and Stahl, Steven A. "Fluency: A Review of Developmental and Remedial Practices. *Journal of Educational Psychology* 95.1 (2003): 3–21.

Lim, Serene and Louis G. Lippman. "Mental Practice and Memorization of Piano Music." *Journal of General Psychology* 118 No. 1 (January 1991): 21–31.

Mallinger, Allan E. and Jeannette De Wyze. *Too Perfect: When Being in Control Gets Out of Control*. New York: Clarkson Potter, 1992.

Malone, Michael S. *The Everything College Survival Book* (2nd Ed.). Massachusetts: 1997

Murphy, Shane M. and Kathleen A. Martin. *Advances in Sport Psychology*, ed. Thelma Horn, 2d ed. Champaign: Human Kinetics Publishers, Inc: 2002, 403–433.

Orman, Suze. "Five Remedies for Couples who Argue About Money" *Yahoo Finance*. Available from http://biz.yahoo.com/pfg/e39couple/arto21.html. Internet. Accessed 5 July 2006.

"Inside the Practice Room." *Percussive Notes* 41 No. 2 (April 2003).

Psychology Today Staff. "Perfectionism: Impossible Dream" [Article, May/June 1995]. *Psychology Today.* Available from http://www.psychologytoday.com/articles/pto-19950501-000002.html. Internet. Accessed 14 June 2006.

Rodriguez, Nancy C. "Success at School: Get Involved Beyond School" [Article, August 1, 2004]. *The Courier-Journal.* Available from http://www.courier-journal.com/cjextra/backtoschool/2004/stories/p11_activities.html. Internet. Accessed 5 July 2006.

Samuels, S. Jay. "Toward a Theory of Automatic Information Processing in Reading, Revisited." *Theoretical Models and Processes of Reading*, 4th ed. Ed. Ruddell, R.B., Ruddell, M.R., & Singer, H. Newark, DE: International Reading Association, 1994. 816–837.

Schultz, Howard and Yang, Dori Jones. *Pour Your Heart Into It: How Starbucks Built a Company One Cup at a Time.* New York: Hyperion, 1997.

"Sexuality" *Harvard University Health Services.* Available from http://huhs.harvard.edu/healthinformation/sexuality.htm. Internet. Accessed 5 July 2006.

Starr, Raymond. "Teaching Study Skills in History Courses." *The History Teacher* 16 No. 4 (August 1983) : 489–504.

Stohrer, Sharon. *The Singer's Companion.* New York: Routledge Taylor and Francis Group, 2006.

Theiler, Anne M. and Louis G. Lippman. "Effects of Mental Practice and Modeling on Guitar and Vocal Performance." *Journal of General Psychology* 122 No. 4 (October 1995) : 329–344.

"Understanding Financial Aid." College Summit & National Endowment for Financial Education. Available from http://www.collegesummit.org/nefe/pages/section2.html. Internet. Accessed 5 July 2006.

University of Texas Southwest Medical Center at Dallas. "The Freshman Fifteen" *annecollins.com.* Available from http://www.annecollins.com/diet-news/freshman-fifteen.htm. Internet. Accessed 5 July 2006.

Wellington, Terra. "Financial Stress Ends With Simple Changes" [Article, June 16, 2003]. *SunCoach: Your Wellness Guide.* Available from http://www.terrawellington.com/Column2003/061603.htm. Internet. Accessed 5 July 2006.

Worthington, Janet Farrar and Farrar, Ronald. *The Ultimate College Survival Guide* (4th Ed.). New Jersey: Peterson's, 1998.

Wren, Sebastian. "Phonics Rules" *Southwest Educational Developmental Laboratory.* Available from http://www.sedl.org/reading/topics/phonicsrules.html. Internet. Accessed 5 June 2006.

about the author

R ich Holly is the Dean of the College of Visual and Performing Arts at Northern Illinois University, one of the most celebrated and comprehensive arts colleges in the United States. He has been a professor of percussion for nearly thirty years, and has served as an academic advisor continuously throughout his career in higher education. As an author and composer he has over one hundred fifty publications in his name, and he has performed and presented workshops throughout North America, Europe and Asia. During the years 2005 and 2006 he served as President of the Percussive Arts Society, and he remains a frequent guest speaker providing motivational and leadership clinics and workshops to music students.